J is for Jump Shot

A Basketball Alphabet

Written by Mike Ulmer and Illustrated by Mark Braught

Sleeping Bear Press™

310 North Main Street, Suite 300
Chelsea, MI 48118
www.sleepingbearpress.com

THOMSON
GALE™

© 2005 Thomson Gale, a part of the Thomson Corporation.

Thomson, Star Logo and Sleeping Bear Press are trademarks
and Gale is a registered trademark used herein under license.

Printed and bound in Canada.

10 9 8 7 6 5 4 3 2 1 (case)
10 9 8 7 6 5 4 3 2 1 (pbk)

Library of Congress Cataloging-in-Publication Data

Ulmer, Michael, 1959-
J is for jump shot : a basketball alphabet / written by Mike Ulmer;
illustrated by Mark Braught.
    p. cm.
Summary: "From A to Z basketball's history, famous players, and the game's
basics such as dribble, pass, and zone are explained using simple rhymes for each
letter topic and expository text filled with details"—Provided by publisher.

pbk ISBN-13: 978-1-58536-338-4   case ISBN-13: 978-1-58536-229-5
     ISBN-10: 1-58536-338-3   ISBN-10: 1-58536-229-8

1. Basketball—Juvenile literature. 2. Alphabet books—Juvenile literature.
I. Braught, Mark, ill. II. Title.
GV885.1.U45 2005
796.323—dc22   2005007319

You can't play basketball without air, in the ball and under your feet. National Basketball Association (NBA) players routinely jump between two and three feet high. Air is great but an air ball isn't. It means your shot missed the rim and the backboard and hit nothing but air.

A is also for assist. An assist is a statistic usually given to the player who passes the ball to a player who then scores. Sometimes, all five players: the center, two guards, and two forwards, will touch the ball before a basket is scored. Players who don't touch the ball contribute by making cuts and setting screens to distract defenders and gain the ballhandler more room to operate. The most successful teams are the ones whose individual members play most unselfishly.

A is for Air.

Put the ball up in the air.
Watch as things take off from there.
You'll be hooked from your first try.
Why just run when you can fly?

Your favorite basketball is like a good friend. You always know where it is and it's always ready to play. Basketballs can be made of leather or synthetic material. Leather balls offer a great surface to grip. Synthetic balls last longer on rougher surfaces. Because the standard rim and basket is always 10 feet high, younger players can use a smaller ball to get their shots to the rim. Basketballs have a circumference of between 29 and 31 inches. Since girls and women usually have smaller hands than men and boys, the ball they use is often a little smaller.

B is also for backboard. The backboard behind the basket can be composed of metal, plastic, and even barnboard. Backboards can be mounted on brick walls, and the side of sheds, on trees and light pole standards. Most backboards are either the 'fan' or the square Plexiglas style. A square, taped or painted on the backboard gives shooters a target. A bank shot, a shot off the backboard, is a great option when trying to shoot the ball past a tall opponent.

B is for Ball.

My favorite ball will usually go
along the perfect path.
It rarely strays; it always stays
exactly where I ask.

B b

C c

A player with the ball who steps on the sideline that runs the length of the court or the baseline that runs along the width of the court is out-of-bounds and must surrender the ball. The court is divided in two by the half-court line. After a basket is scored, the opposing team usually has 10 seconds to advance the ball over the half-court line. When a shooter hits a jump shot from behind the three-point line, his team is awarded three, not two points. The three-point line is an arced line that begins and ends on the baseline and is 19 feet, 9 inches from the center of the basket. (In the NBA, the distance is 22 feet.) The three-pointer is a great way to make up ground if your team is way behind.

C is also for center. The center is at the middle of the defense. Guards are usually stationed at the top of the key with forwards at the back near the basket and the baseline.

C is for Court.

I watch where I am going,
and to avoid mistakes
I keep the lines in mind
with every step I take.

In basketball, everyone has to know how to dribble. Other than passing the ball, the only way to move the ball upcourt is to dribble it. There are all kinds of dribbles, the crossover dribble in which you change the hand that dribbles the ball (to keep it away from an opponent) or an around-the-back or even through-the-legs dribble. Remember, to double dribble—to dribble, pick up the ball with both hands and start dribbling again—is an infraction.

D also stands for defense. Good defensive players use balance, anticipation, and short, fast steps to challenge and head off offensive players. They try not to surrender good position near their basket and control rebounds by "boxing out" or putting them-selves between the rebound and the offensive player.

D
d

D is for Dribble.

Give me the ball; start the show.
Watch me dribble; here I go.
Dribbling is the greatest fun.
I can get past anyone.

E e

E is for Energy.

Yours can be the gift of hustle.
Skill is just one part of the mix.
Don't forget to bring the energy,
when your whole team needs a lift.

Every good team has what a coach calls an energy player. Energy players run harder and dive for loose balls. Often their aggressive play and quick movements spark other teammates to work harder. They hustle on defense and go for every rebound. She also works to get opposing players on offense to commit charging fouls. Charging fouls are called when an offensive player runs into a defensive player who has established her position by setting her feet. They make sure the coach notices them at every practice and tryout.

E is also for equipment. Unlike football and hockey, basketball doesn't require much padding or equipment. All you need to play is a backboard, hoop, and ball.

F is for Fast Break.

Every time you turn around,
we're on the run and basket bound.
We never pause or hesitate;
we put the fast in the fast break.

The key to the fast break is to go from defense to offense so quickly that your opponent doesn't have time to set up on defense. Every fast break starts with a defensive rebound and a first pass or outlet pass to a player who can advance the ball.

In a three-on-two fast break, three offensive players attack a basket defended by two defensive players. In this formation, a player on each side or wing runs a little ahead of the ballhandler who dribbles the ball down the middle of the court. On a two-on-one break, the goal of the ballhandler is to try to get the lone defender to commit to either him or his teammate, leaving one player open to take the ball to the basket and score.

F also stands for free throw or foul shot. A free throw is an uncontested shot from the free throw line. It is awarded to the player who was fouled. If you're standing at the free throw line and wondering how far you are from the basket, the answer is exactly 13 feet. A successful foul shot that goes in is worth one point. If a player was fouled in the act of shooting, he is given two free shots. If a player is fouled while shooting and the shot still goes in, he is awarded a free throw and the chance of making a three-point play. A player fouled while shooting a three can add a free throw for a four-point play.

Ff

G is for Globetrotters.

They come and travel to your town
and make you laugh and clown around.
Their own home court, they've never seen,
but each night they're the hometown team.

In one 38-year stretch, the Harlem Globetrotters lost twice and once put together a winning streak of 1,270 games. Abe Saperstein was coaching a team in Chicago called the Savoy Big Five. In 1937 when the Savoy Ballroom on Chicago's South Side decided it no longer wanted to sponsor a team, Saperstein renamed the club the Harlem Globetrotters, took the 'Trotters on the road and eventually changed the focus to fun and entertainment.

The Globetrotters' most famous trick is the Magic Circle ballhandling routine. The Globetrotters' shooting, dribbling, and weaving magic make them a delight to watch. The 'Trotters also play more serious competitive games against college teams.

Wilt "The Stilt" Chamberlain was one of the most famous Harlem Globetrotters. The 7'-1" center began his professional career in 1958 when the Globetrotters signed him. Wilt holds the NBA single-game record for points in one game (100, March 2, 1962) against the New York Knicks.

H is for Hoosier.

In Indiana each dad and mother
has hit a jump shot at the buzzer.
Yes, every Hoosier, gramp or tot,
will always hit the open shot.

H h

Not every one of Indiana's six million people play basketball but it's no exaggeration to call Indiana America's basketball state. Indiana-born basketball stars include Boston Celtic great Larry Bird and Stephanie White-McCarty, who scored 2,869 points playing for Purdue University in West Lafayette, Indiana.

H is also for height. Michael Jordan went from 5' 10" in his sophomore year in high school to 6' 6" by the end of his sophomore year at college. There was no other member of his family over 6' tall. His brother Larry is 5' 6". Being tall is an advantage in basketball, but there is plenty of room for smaller, faster players too. Centers are usually the tallest players, followed by forwards. Guards, who depend on quickness and have less rebounding responsibility, are usually smaller.

I is for Improve.

Get better one level at a time.
In every single way
the question you must always ask:
"Did I improve today?"

The best way to improve is to work on things that you aren't good at. For example, if you are right-handed, your dribble with your right hand is probably fine. If you want to improve, work on your left-hand dribble and your left-hand layup.

Focus on the next stage of your improvement. If you have trouble with free throws set yourself a target of hitting 10 in a row after practice—then 20 or 30. That's what the pros do. If you need to improve on facing the basket, get a friend to throw you passes and practice taking your first step toward the basket after catching the ball. The only thing that determines how much you improve is how much and how hard you practice.

Ii

J is for Jump shot.

It's easy to get your jump shot right—
just practice morning, noon, and night.
And keep in mind the golden rule:
do not neglect the follow-through.

The jump shot is the most common shot in basketball. By jumping as the ball is released, the shooter makes the shot harder to block. Here are a few tips. When you release the ball, the shooting hand should be the only one in contact with the ball. Flipping the wrist in the follow-through will create backspin. That's important because the ball needs to clear the rim before it can fall in. Much of the energy for the jump shot should come from the large muscles in the legs and back. Don't forget to look at your target. Some coaches advise shooters to look at the back of the rim, others to concentrate on the imaginary cylinder above the rim.

With a hook shot, the player uses one arm to gain space and releases the ball in an arc above his head. It's a handy shot when there are opposing players who are close enough to block a jump shot.

J is also for jump ball. Each game begins with a jump ball in the center of the court where two players from opposing teams try to tip the ball to a teammate.

K k

K is for Key.

I can't do much in just three ticks.
It goes too fast for me.
But it's all the time I ever get
to get out of the key.

To make sure they don't get an unfair advantage, offensive players aren't allowed to spend too long under the other team's basket. Players can move through the key from one side of the court to the other in an effort to beat the defense and be open to accept a pass. If the official notices a player in the key for more than three seconds, he will (call a three second violation) and award the opposite team the ball.

The key is an area of the court that is usually 19' long and 12' wide. To make it easy to spot a player in or out of the key, it is painted a different color than the rest of the floor. That's why the key is also called the paint.

K is also for Kareem Abdul-Jabbar. A star with the Milwaukee Bucks and Los Angeles Lakers, Abdul-Jabbar scored more points, blocked more shots, won more MVP awards, and played in more All-Star Games than any other NBA player.

Often, the closer you get to the basket, the tougher it is to take an open shot. That's why players need to hit their layups when they find themselves with a clear route to the basket. Many beginners let go of the ball when they're directly under the basket instead of a step or two before. Using the backboard also helps.

L is also for language. Basketball has a language all its own. A trey is a three-point shot. If you knock down a deuce, you've scored a two-pointer. To hit the line is to shoot a foul shot. The free throw line is sometimes called the charity stripe. A dunk is a jam and a player who scores in the clutch is money.

L is for Layup.

It seems like such an easy thing.
Just lay it up and lay it in.
But when you finally reach the hoop
you're usually working in a group.

L l

M is for March Madness.

A month devoted to college hoops
and upsets, wins, and sadness.
It happens every single year
this thing they call March Madness.

March Madness, the National Collegiate Athletic Association (NCAA) championship tournament is the highlight of the men's and women's college basketball season.

Sixty-four teams from across America face off for the chance to win the national championship in the month-long tournament. The women's championship also features a 64-team draw.

In Canada, the men's team that wins the CIS, or the Canadian Interuniversity Sports tournament in Halifax, Nova Scotia, wins the national title. The women's tournament is held in a different city every year.

M also stands for matchups. If a player is taller or faster than an opponent, the coach runs plays designed to get the ball to the player with the advantage.

M m

N n

N is for NBA.

Divided into 30 teams
are countless hopes and countless dreams;
to be a star in the NBA
is something you might do someday.

The National Basketball Association, commonly known as the NBA, was formed in 1949 and offers the best professional basketball in the world. It includes 30 teams, including one in Canada, the Toronto Raptors. NBA stars include LeBron James of the Cleveland Cavaliers, Carmelo Anthony of the Denver Nuggets, and Miami Heat star Shaquille O'Neal. The Boston Celtics have won the NBA championship a record 16 times. Next are the Los Angeles Lakers with 14 titles. The Lakers own the NBA's best-ever winning streak, a 33-gamer in the 1971-72 season.

N also stands for nations. Players now come from around the world to play in the NBA. Yao Ming of the Houston Rockets is from China. Dallas star Dirk Nowitzki came to the league from Germany. Steve Nash of the Phoenix Suns is Canadian, while Utah star Andrei Kirilenko grew up in Russia. National teams from Europe and South America are among the very best in the world.

N is also for net. Nets can be made of twine, nylon, or even metal. There is no sweeter feeling than a shot so perfect it hits "nothing but net" or "nothing but nylon."

Playing one-on-one is, just as it sounds, one player playing basketball against another. Players can sharpen both their offensive and defensive skills. Dribbling with the ball to the basket and scoring or going after the rebound, and taking another shot are important skills when playing one-on-one. A great one-on-one player drives to the basket and goes for the rebounds if he misses.

O also stands for offense. Some teams rely on the fast break or transition game. Others prefer moving the ball more methodically up the floor and initiating a half-court offense. When designing an offense, coaches use numbers to represent positions. Number one is the point guard who calls out plays. Then comes the number two or shooting guard. A small forward is number three. A bigger, power forward is number four and the center is number five.

O also stands for Olympics. Men's basketball has been played at the Olympics since 1936. Women's basketball has been a part of the games since the 1976 Olympics in Montreal.

O o

O is for One-on-One.

I don't always need a league
with coaches, rules, and referees.
I can have a pile of fun
just playing my buddies one-on-one.

P p

Passing or dishing the ball is one of the most expressive and fun parts of playing basketball. The baseball-style pass as well as the chest pass are considered the most dependable. The bounce pass is an essential and underused weapon. Some of the showier passes include the behind-the-back or no-look pass and the alley-oop in which the ball is tossed up near the basket for a teammate to slam home. Los Angeles Laker star Magic Johnson is considered to be the greatest passer in NBA history.

P also stands for press. In the half-court or full-court press, defensive teams assign two players or double-team the ballhandler to force errors.

P is for Pass.

Baseball, bounce, or alley-oop,
over the head or underhand scoop,
Name a time or situation—
there's a pass for the occasion.

NBA games are divided into four 12-minute quarters with half-time between the second and third quarters. College, Women's National Basketball Association (WNBA) games, and adult games played in many countries outside the United States are routinely broken down into four 10-minute quarters. High school games are usually divided into four eight-minute quarters.

You know the quarter has expired when the buzzer goes off. The buzzer is activated automatically or by the scoreboard operator. The buzzer is also used to signal substitutions and the end of time-outs.

Q is for Quarters.
Just because they're all called quarters,
doesn't mean they're all the same.
Quarters come in different measures,
Depending on the type of game.

R is for Rebound.

I take my fun right off the rack.
You put it up; I'll get it back.
No shot too short or too off-line
for me to rebound every time.

Any shot that hits the backboard or rim and doesn't go in is called a rebound. Since more shots are missed than made in nearly every game, rebounding is one of the game's most important skills. A rebounder needs to be aggressive. Knowing when to jump is more important than how high a player can jump. The best rebounders grab the ball at the top of their jump and use elbows, shoulders, and body to shield the ball from her opponents. A good rebounder can guess where the ball will land and get to that point before an opponent.

S is for Signal.

Hands on hips or on the head,
maybe chop the air instead.
A pretty good ref I could make
if I could keep the signals straight.

Basketball games are officiated by crews of two or three referees, each with equal authority. Officials must enforce the rules, oversee the flow of substitutions, and make sure the game starts on time. That leaves a lot of decisions to communicate to players, coaches, and spectators and that's why referees use signals.

When a referee signals with his hands on hips, he is calling a blocking foul on a player who has illegally impeded another player. When he puts his palm on his head, he is signaling a 24-second violation against a team that has not generated a shot in the maximum time they are allowed. When he chops the air, he is signaling time in and asking the scorer's table to start the clock. An official also signals with his fingers to indicate the number of the player who has earned a foul.

S is also for statistics. Statistic sheets or stat sheets are kept by scorekeepers at the scorer's table. The scorers keep a running tally of the score and record who has how many points and how many fouls.

If a player with the ball takes more than one step without dribbling, she is called for traveling and must surrender the ball to the other team. This results in another **T** word: a turnover.

The key to gaining space and moving without traveling is the use of the pivot foot. Remember, one foot has to stay on the ground but the player can still rotate on his pivot foot to gain room for a shot or a pass. If he moves his pivot foot, he will be called for traveling. When a player picks up the ball with both hands and uses his pivot foot, he has 'killed' or ended his dribble.

T stands for time-out. When a coach calls a time-out, she usually asks his team to run a play they have practiced.

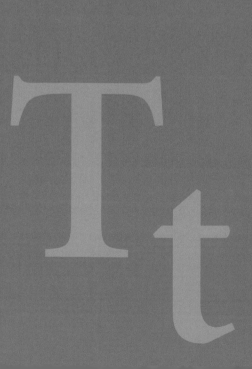

T is for Traveling.

If you take steps and have the ball
expect to get a traveling call.
The dribble is the way to be
a player who is travel free.

While basketball teams or schools rarely change their colors, uniform fashions change. It once was popular to wear a T-shirt under a jersey and socks that stretched all the way up to a player's knee. The style of uniforms has changed from tight and stretchy in the 1970s and 1980s to the baggy style still popular today. Each uniform bears a number and a player's number is their identity. Players often choose numbers they have worn since they were small or wear the numbers of their favorite players.

Michael Jordan's numbers (he wore 23 and 45) are among the most famous numbers in basketball history. So is the number 6 worn by NBA stars Bill Russell and Julius Erving.

U is for Uniform.

You are bearing special colors—
be they silver, gold, or blue.
You're a member of a family
so take pride in what you do.

V v

Cutting down the net has long been a championship tradition in basketball. Usually, every player cuts a strand until the net comes free as a permanent souvenir. Players who have won championships usually don't remember the plays or the moments that went into the victory. What stays with them forever is the friendships and the feeling that came with pooling everyone's talents to create a great team.

V is for Victory.

You won't recall every ball game.
There are wins you will forget.
But I'm betting you'll remember
the magic time you cut the net.

W is for WNBA.

Women come from around the globe
to show the skills they learned at home.
There is a place for the best to play—
it's called the WNBA

Since its debut in 1997, the Women's National Basketball Association (WNBA) has been home to the world's best basketball players from Cynthia Cooper to Chamique Holdsclaw to up-and-coming talents Diana Taurasi, Alana Beard, and Lindsay Whalen. The WNBA began its first season with eight teams and now boasts 13 clubs in Charlotte, Southern Connecticut, Detroit, Houston, Indianapolis, Los Angeles, Minneapolis, New York City, Phoenix, Sacramento, San Antonio, Seattle, and Washington.

W is also for Wooden and Wilkens. Lenny Wilkens and John Wooden are enshrined both as players and coaches in the Basketball Hall of Fame in Springfield, Massachusetts. Wooden was a star at the University of Purdue and a one-time College Player of the Year who coached UCLA to 10 national championships. A terrific point guard, Lenny Wilkens was named one of the NBA's 50 greatest players ever. He holds the record for most wins by an NBA coach.

W
W

Whoever invented the idea of making one team **X**s and one team **O**s should have a plaque in the coach's hall of fame. **O**s are offensive players. **X**s are defensive players. Coaches will use anything to diagram a play, a chalkboard, a wipe-off plastic board, a napkin, or program. Coaches have special plays to inbound the ball when there is little time left and often design plays on the spot to use in special situations.

X is for Xs and Os.

If you served her alphabet soup
and gave my coach her druthers
she would keep every X and O
and throw out all the others.

X
x

Yy

Each day, basketball games are played on the gym floors of the more than 2,400 YMCAs in America. Basketball was invented in 1891 by Dr. James Naismith, a Canadian-born instructor working at the YMCA Training School (now Springfield College) in Springfield, Massachusetts. He had been asked to concoct a game to keep students active through the winter. There was an elevated running track 10 feet above the floor. Naismith asked the custodian, Pop Stebbins, to get a pair of boxes a little bit bigger than a soccer ball and nail them to the facing of the running track. Pop Stebbins returned to the gym with a pair of peach baskets and the game was born.

According to the game's original 13 rules, if a game ended in a tie, the first team to score in extra time was a winner. Three consecutive fouls also resulted in a score for the opposition.

Y is for YMCA.

There is a game going on right now
in many cities and lots of towns.
There's always a place for you to play.
Just find your local YMCA

In a zone defense, the floor is divided up with every player assigned an area on the floor to guard. There are several types of zones including the 3-2 zone in which three defenders are positioned across the court in front of the foul circle and two near the net. In a 2-3 zone, the 2 defenders are out in front and 3 are nearer the basket. Coaches will change defenses, sometimes from moment to moment, in an effort to make their teams harder to score against.

When a player guards a counterpart on the other team rather than a space on the floor, it is usually called man-to-man defense, even when females are playing.

Z z

Z is for Zone.

See this spot, right over here?
I'll defend it, never fear.
Now, that area atop the key
becomes your responsibility.

Mike Ulmer

When he isn't shooting hoops with daughter Hannah at home in Hamilton, Ontario, Canada, Mike writes a sports column for the *Toronto Sun* newspaper. He has written four best-selling books about hockey and *J is for Jump Shot* is his fourth children's book. Mike also wrote *M is for Maple: A Canadian Alphabet*; *H is for Horse: An Equestrian Alphabet*; and *The Gift of the Inuksuk*. Mike is married to journalist Agnes Bongers. Their oldest daughter Sadie prefers horses to dribbling, while young Madalyn hasn't quite made up her mind.

Mark Braught

Mark Braught's 25 years of professional experience have earned him prestigious awards from the American Advertising Federation (ADDY), *Communication Arts*, the NY Art Directors Club, and the Society of Illustrators among others. He received his degree in graphic design from Indiana State University, and attended the Minneapolis College of Art & Design. He lives in Commerce, Georgia, with his wife Laura, their five cats, and Charlie the dog.

He also illustrated *T is for Touchdown: A Football Alphabet*; *P is for Peach: A Georgia Alphabet*, and *Cosmo's Moon*, all published by Sleeping Bear Press.